Thank you for purchasing this book! Please consider leaving us a review on Amazon if you enjoyed it. It will help us greatly in helping other readers find our books and allow us to continue to publish high quality content for our readers. Thank you for your support!

Rylan lolo

Made in United States
Troutdale, OR
12/08/2023

15534455R00058